ANIMAL ORIGAMI

Fumiaki Shingu

Mud Puddle inc.
NEW YORK

W9-AYD-258

Animal Origami
Created by Fumiaki Shingu

© 2006 by Mud Puddle, Inc.

Mud Puddle, Inc.
36 W. 25th Street
New York, NY 10010
info@mudpuddleinc.com

ISBN: 978-1-60311-105-8

Printed and bound in China

CONTENTS

★ Very Easy

★★ Easy

★★★ More Difficult

INTRODUCTION

THE MAGICAL WORLD OF ORIGAMI

Picture a square piece of paper.

Imagine that square piece of paper turning into an animal, a flower, a box or something that moves.

This is the timeless appeal of origami, the Japanese art of paper folding. Origami has been captivating people and holding them spellbound for more than a thousand years. It's believed that by folding, decorating and playing with paper you cultivate your creativity and spark your imagination.

It's easy to master the techniques of origami and, by practicing as much as you can, you develop your skills and quickly move on to more advanced steps and projects.

This book can be used by beginners and experts alike. The projects are classified according to their level of difficulty. Children and adults will readily find projects that match their skills.

It makes me very happy to share my origami experiences with you and I would be so pleased if my origami techniques provide you with joy and delight.

—Fumiaki Shingu
Tokyo 2006

EXPLANATION OF DIAGRAMS

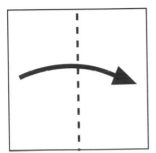 

Fold on the dotted line.

Fold backward on the dotted line.

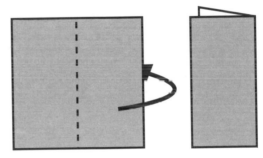

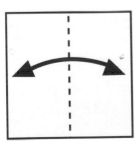 

Fold to make a crease and fold back.

5

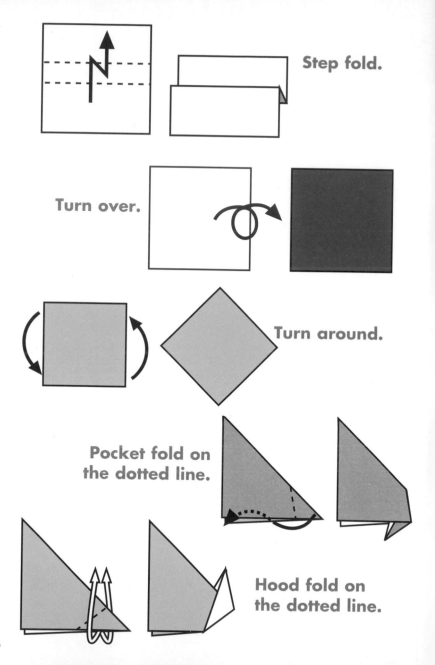

Step fold.

Turn over.

Turn around.

Pocket fold on the dotted line.

Hood fold on the dotted line.

6

Take time to practice and master the three basic folds described here. They are used throughout this book and will allow you to create the beautiful projects that follow.

Step Fold

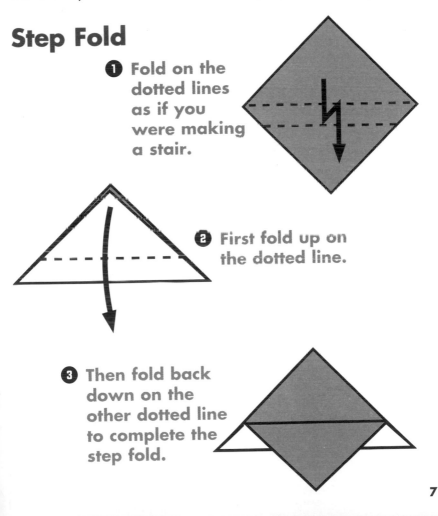

1 Fold on the dotted lines as if you were making a stair.

2 First fold up on the dotted line.

3 Then fold back down on the other dotted line to complete the step fold.

Pocket Fold

Hood Fold

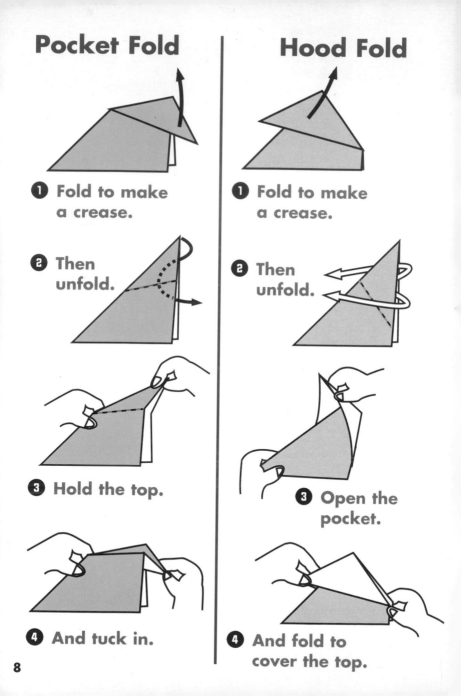

1 Fold to make a crease.

1 Fold to make a crease.

2 Then unfold.

2 Then unfold.

3 Hold the top.

3 Open the pocket.

4 And tuck in.

4 And fold to cover the top.

8

FOX FACE ★

1 Fold in half.

2 Fold on the dotted line.

3 Turn over.

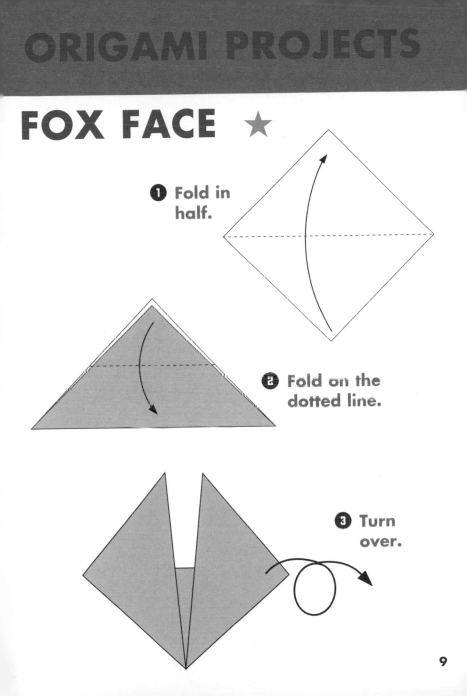

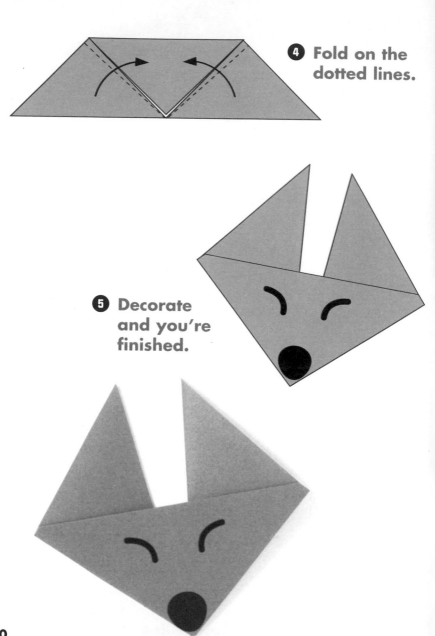

4 Fold on the dotted lines.

5 Decorate and you're finished.

RABBIT FACE ★

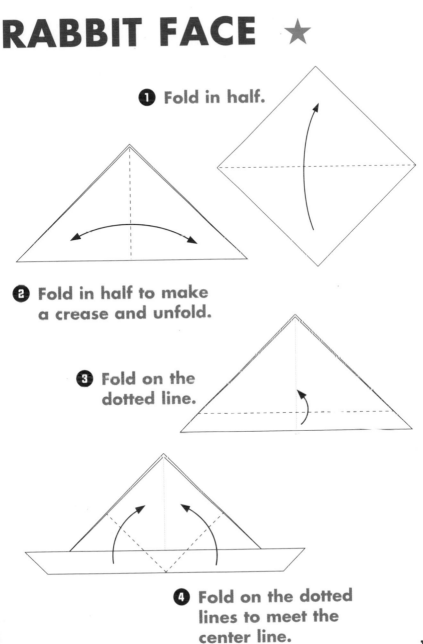

1 Fold in half.

2 Fold in half to make a crease and unfold.

3 Fold on the dotted line.

4 Fold on the dotted lines to meet the center line.

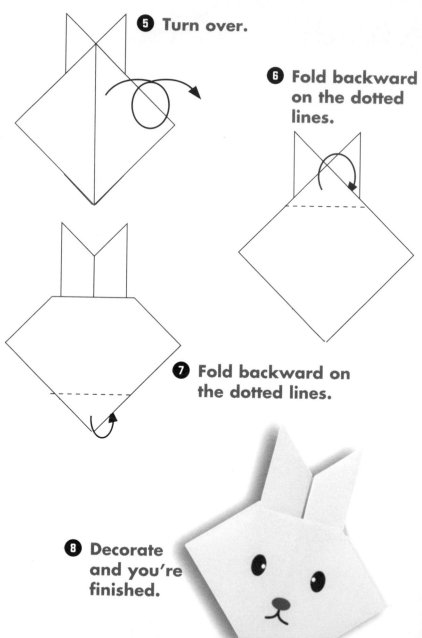

❺ Turn over.

❻ Fold backward on the dotted lines.

❼ Fold backward on the dotted lines.

❽ Decorate and you're finished.

12

SWAN ★★

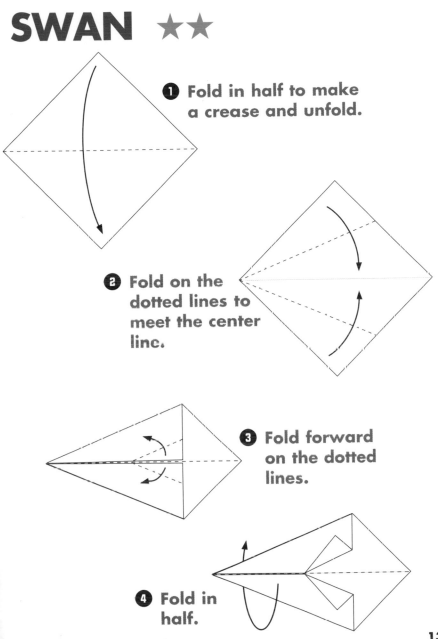

1 Fold in half to make a crease and unfold.

2 Fold on the dotted lines to meet the center line.

3 Fold forward on the dotted lines.

4 Fold in half.

13

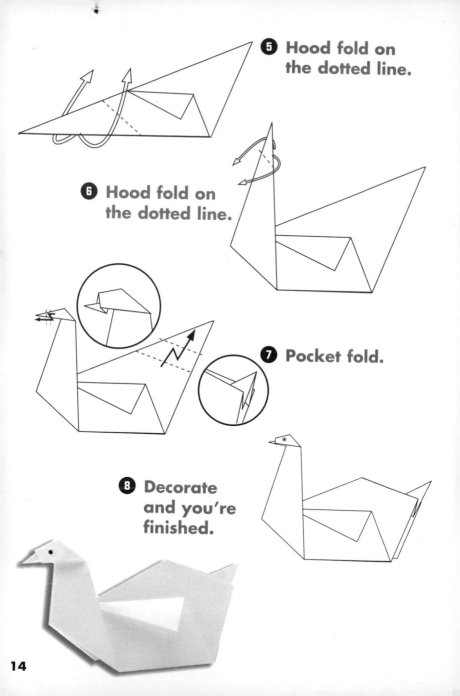

5 Hood fold on the dotted line.

6 Hood fold on the dotted line.

7 Pocket fold.

8 Decorate and you're finished.

GIRAFFE ★★

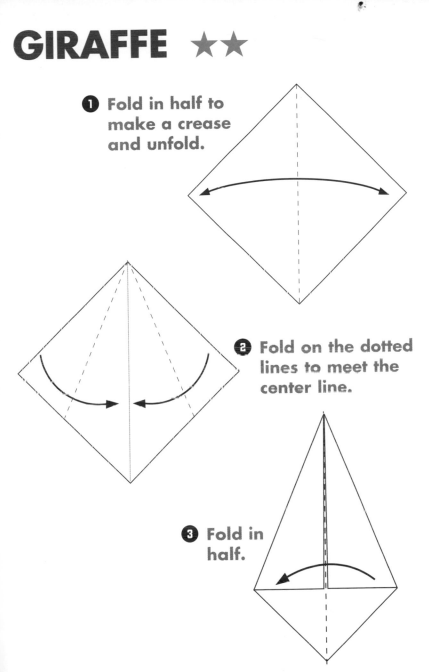

1 Fold in half to make a crease and unfold.

2 Fold on the dotted lines to meet the center line.

3 Fold in half.

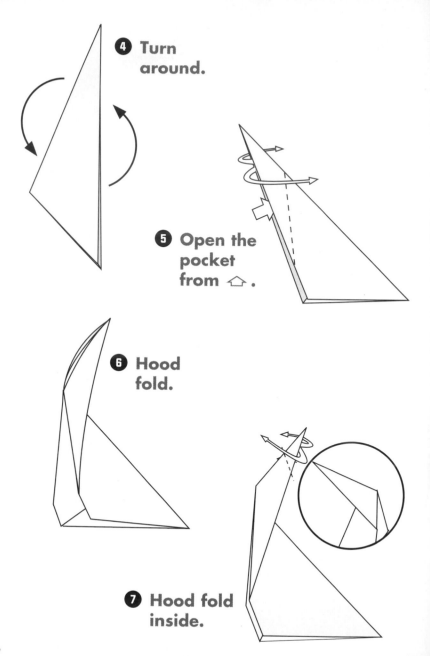

4 Turn around.

5 Open the pocket from ⌂.

6 Hood fold.

7 Hood fold inside.

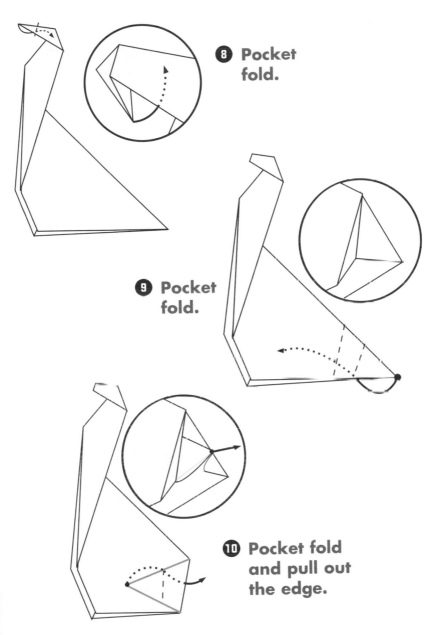

8 Pocket fold.

9 Pocket fold.

10 Pocket fold and pull out the edge.

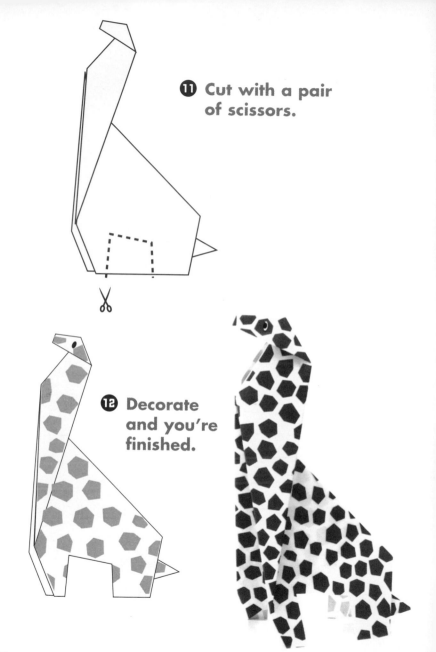

⑪ Cut with a pair of scissors.

⑫ Decorate and you're finished.

PIG ★★

1 Fold on the dotted lines to meet the center line.

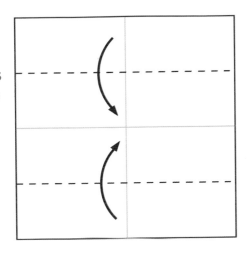

2 Fold on the dotted lines to make creases and unfold.

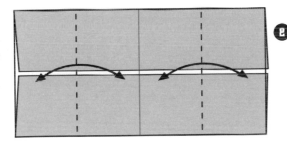

3 Fold forward on the dotted lines.

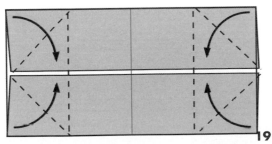

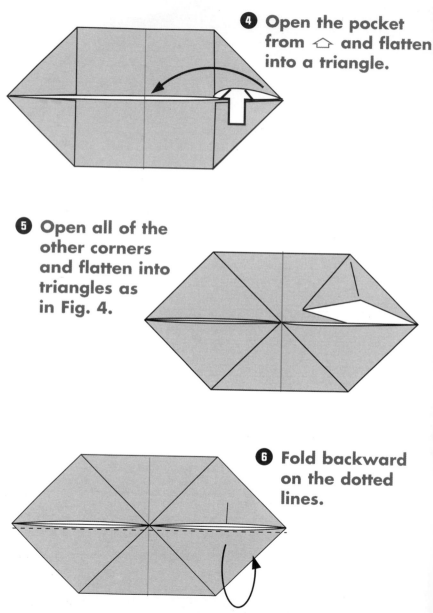

4 Open the pocket from ⬠ and flatten into a triangle.

5 Open all of the other corners and flatten into triangles as in Fig. 4.

6 Fold backward on the dotted lines.

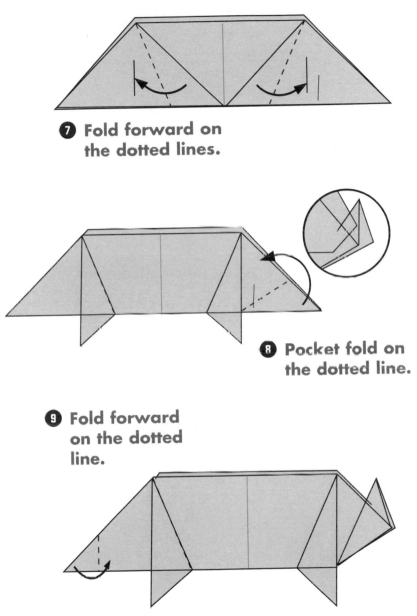

7 Fold forward on the dotted lines.

8 Pocket fold on the dotted line.

9 Fold forward on the dotted line.

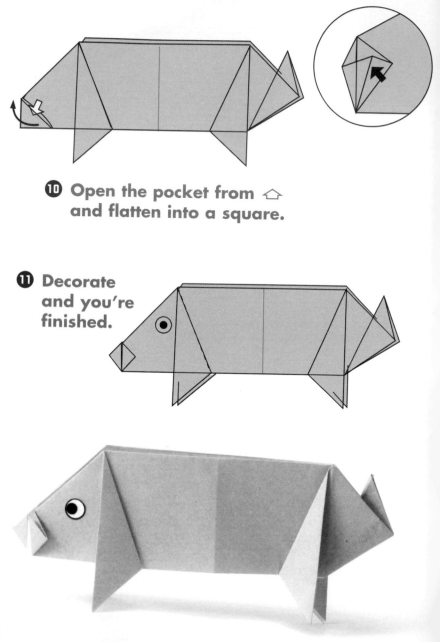

10 Open the pocket from 🏠 and flatten into a square.

11 Decorate and you're finished.

WHALE ★★

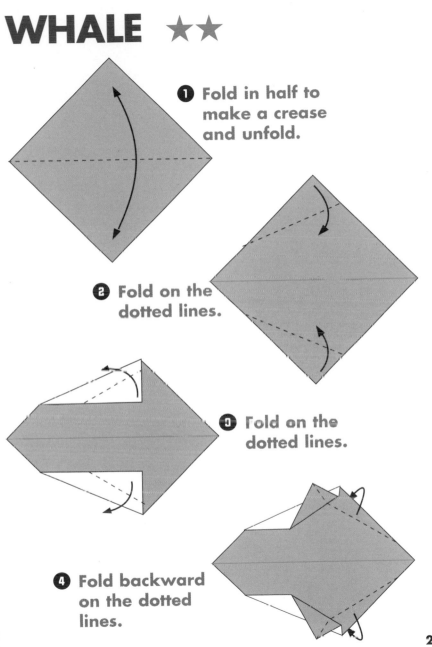

1 Fold in half to make a crease and unfold.

2 Fold on the dotted lines.

3 Fold on the dotted lines.

4 Fold backward on the dotted lines.

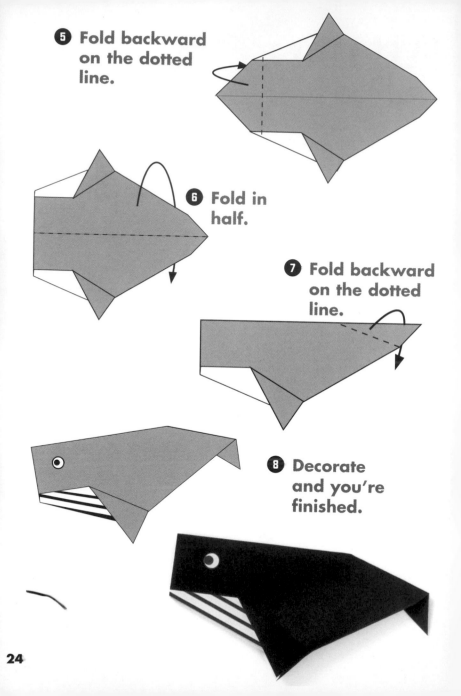

5 Fold backward on the dotted line.

6 Fold in half.

7 Fold backward on the dotted line.

8 Decorate and you're finished.

24

ELEPHANT ★★★

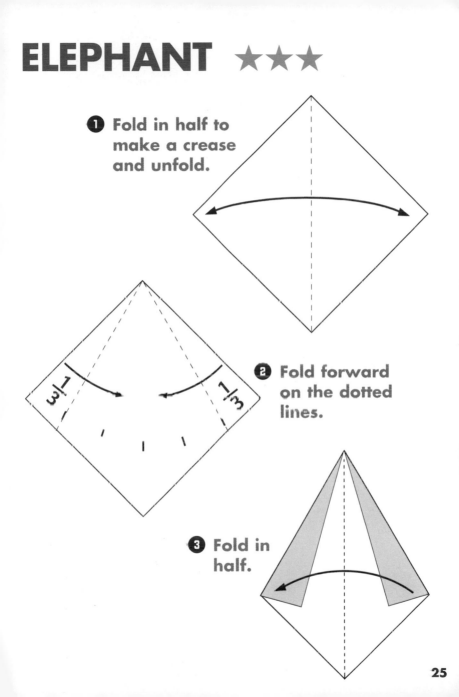

❶ Fold in half to make a crease and unfold.

$\frac{1}{3}$ | $\frac{1}{3}$

❷ Fold forward on the dotted lines.

❸ Fold in half.

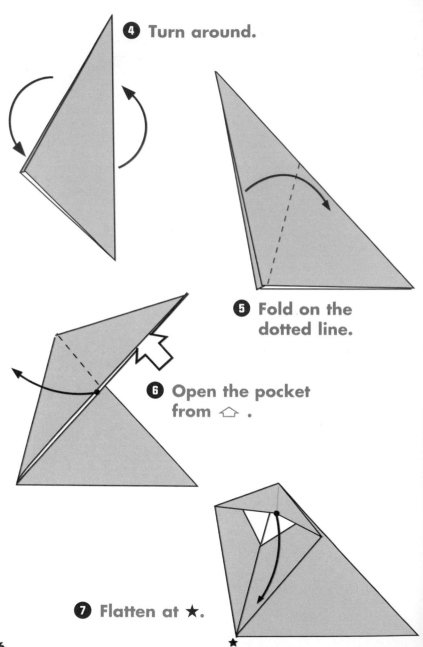

4 Turn around.

5 Fold on the dotted line.

6 Open the pocket from ⌂ .

7 Flatten at ★.

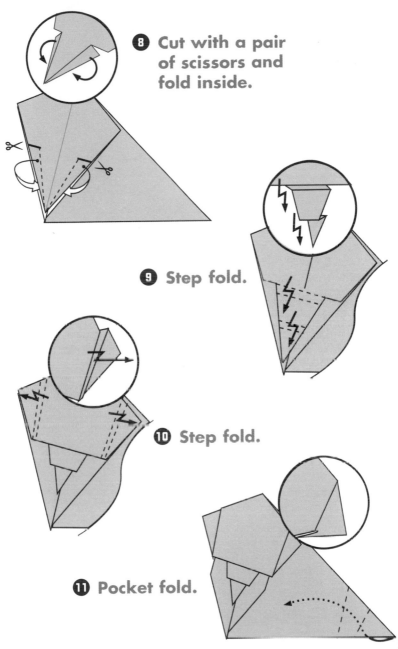

❽ Cut with a pair of scissors and fold inside.

❾ Step fold.

❿ Step fold.

⓫ Pocket fold.

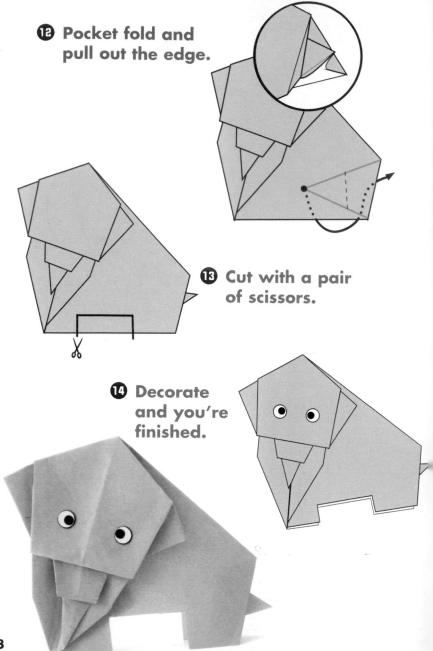

⑫ Pocket fold and pull out the edge.

⑬ Cut with a pair of scissors.

⑭ Decorate and you're finished.

PANTHER  ★ ★ ★

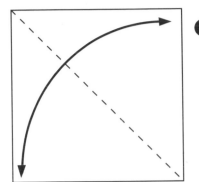

❶ Fold in half to make a crease and unfold.

❷ Fold on the dotted lines to meet the center line.

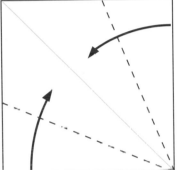

❸ Turn over.

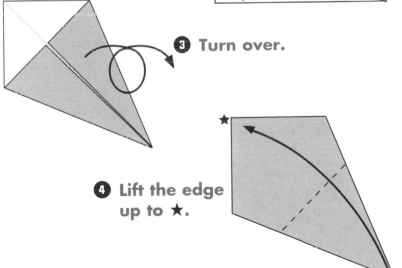

❹ Lift the edge up to ★.

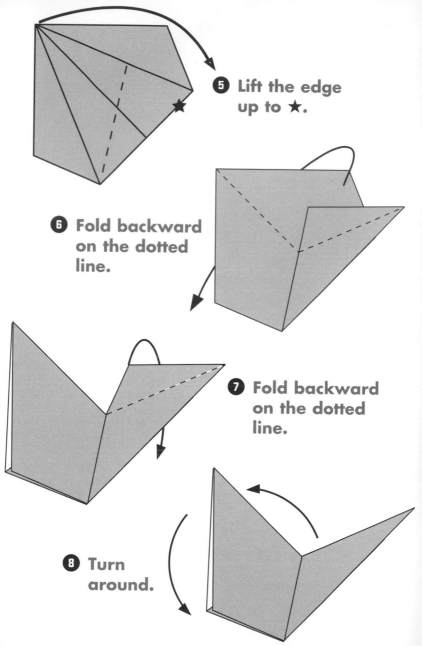

⑤ Lift the edge up to ★.

⑥ Fold backward on the dotted line.

⑦ Fold backward on the dotted line.

⑧ Turn around.

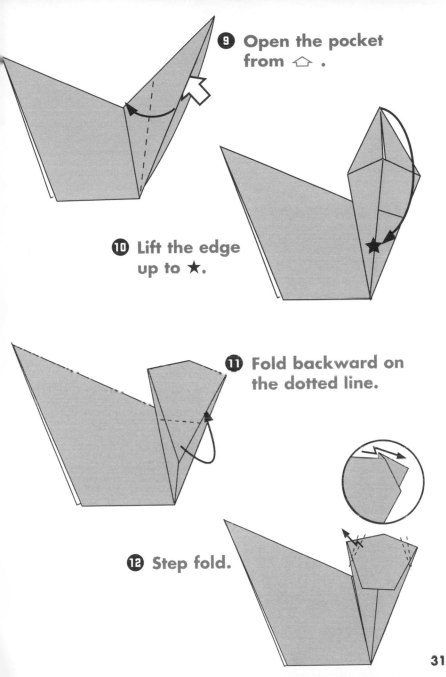

9 Open the pocket from ⌂ .

10 Lift the edge up to ★.

11 Fold backward on the dotted line.

12 Step fold.

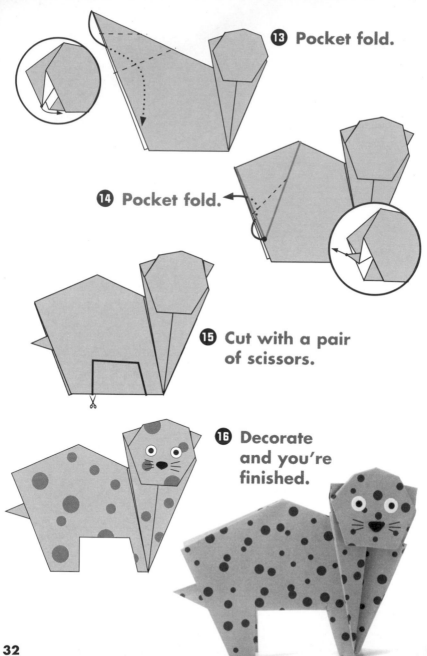

⓭ Pocket fold.

⓮ Pocket fold.

⓯ Cut with a pair of scissors.

⓰ Decorate and you're finished.